Retreats

—

Fast Track to Freedom

—

A Guide for Leaders and Practitioners

Yogani

From The AYP Enlightenment Series

Copyright © 2012 by Yogani

All rights reserved.

July 2012 Edition

Advanced Yoga Practices (AYP)

For ordering information go to:

www.advancedyogapractices.com

ISBN 978-1-4781380-6-8 (Paperback)
ISBN 978-0-9819255-6-1 (eBook)

This is dedicated to all who gather together
for their spiritual progress,
and for the betterment of humanity.

Introduction

Since Advanced Yoga Practices (AYP) was started in 2003, the number of people utilizing this open source system of full-scope yoga practices has grown steadily around the world. It has evolved from being primarily an internet resource to a shelf-full of books, and now to increasing "real-world" activities including meditation groups, hands-on training, and retreats organized and run by those who choose to share the knowledge and experiences that come with the effective application of the practices. I am most grateful to all who have been sharing the knowledge for the benefit of others.

This small volume has been written to provide guidelines for assisting those who wish to organize and implement AYP retreats. It is also for those interested in attending retreats for personal benefit and for benefiting the world with the cultivation of abiding inner silence, and its natural application in daily living. The experience with AYP retreats has been very good, and this book is offered in the hope that many more retreats will be conducted around the world.

The AYP Enlightenment Series is an endeavor to present the most effective methods of spiritual practice in a series of easy-to-read books that anyone can use to gain practical results immediately and over the long term. For centuries, many of these powerful practices have been shrouded in secrecy, mainly in an effort to preserve them. Now we find ourselves in the *information age*, and able to preserve knowledge for present and future generations like never before. The question remains: "How far can we go in effectively transmitting spiritual methods in writing?"

Since the beginning, the writings of AYP have been an experiment to see just how much can be conveyed, with much more detail included on practices than in the spiritual writings of the past Can books provide us the specific means necessary to tread the path to enlightenment, or do we have to surrender at the feet of a *guru* to find our salvation? Well, clearly we must surrender to something, even if it is to our own innate potential to live a freer and happier life. If we are able to do that, and maintain regular practice, then books like this one can come alive and instruct us in the ways of human spiritual transformation. If the reader is ready and the book is worthy, amazing things can happen.

While one person's name is given as the author of this book, it is actually a distillation of the efforts of thousands of practitioners over thousands of years. This is one person's attempt to simplify and make practical the spiritual methods that many have demonstrated throughout history. All who have gone before have my deepest gratitude, as do the many I am privileged to be in touch with in the present who continue to practice with dedication and good results.

I hope you will find this book to be a useful resource as you travel along your chosen path.

Practice wisely, and enjoy!

Table of Contents

Chapter 1 – Why Retreats? 1

    Retreat Basics 3
    The Magic of Group Practice 5
    Short Term and Long Term Benefits 8

Chapter 2 – Retreat Implementation 9

    Types of Retreats 10
    Retreat Structure and Schedule 20
    Planning and Running Retreats 25
    Questions, Cautions and Safety Measures 42
    A Typical Day on a Retreat 64
    Transitioning Back to Normal Daily Activity 71

Chapter 3 – The Inner Dynamics 75

    Reviewing the Core Practices 75
    What Happens to Us on Retreat? 84
    Experiences – Signs of Purification and Opening 86
    Uplifting Effects on the Surroundings 92
    Lasting Cumulative Benefits 93

Chapter 4 – Bringing it Home 97

    The Rise of Abiding Inner Silence 97
    A Happier Way of Living 99

Further Reading and Support 101

Chapter 1 – Why Retreats?

When we begin practicing twice-daily deep meditation, and after some time add on spinal breathing pranayama, there may come a desire to increase our practice time beyond the normal twice-daily 20-30 minutes per session for faster results. Once we have had a taste of that expansive blissful silence within us, and the ecstatic sensations that often come with it, we want more, much more. So what can we do?

Our first impulse may be to increase the time of our sittings – more practice will yield more of those good results, right? More is better!

But if we do this, increase our meditation time beyond 20 minutes and spinal breathing beyond 10 minutes, we will soon find that there is only so much purification and opening our nervous system can handle on any given day, or in any given week. The result? Symptoms of overload, which can bring physical, mental and emotional discomfort, until we can rebalance our practice routine in relation to the reality of our inner capacity for change and the responsibilities we have in daily life.

Having tried that, we may then try adding on more of the AYP practices before we are ready, with similar results. There are plenty available in the AYP writings. However, if we try to build our practice too quickly, we will find that Rome was not built in a day, and neither is our transformation to a life in abiding inner silence, ecstatic bliss, and the unity of constant outpouring divine love.

Nevertheless our bhakti (spiritual desire) may well be surging all the same, and we have to do something to advance along our path. There is no time to lose.

So what can we do? First, wherever we are in taking on spiritual practices, we should stabilize our daily sittings at a level that is comfortable for our individual characteristics of purification and opening. We call this "self-pacing." And second, we should introduce any additions in practices one at a time in a measured way, so as to avoid the excesses that can occur when we rush ahead too fast.

Finally, we should consider going on a retreat. Not just any retreat, though there are many kinds that can be beneficial, but an AYP retreat, which can add a great leap in our progress, without the symptoms of overdoing that can occur when we try to move ahead too fast with our practices at home. This is accomplished with precise scheduling of multiple practice sessions in a group setting, balanced with light activity in the form of meetings, meals and walking. With all of our needs attended to in a well-organized retreat environment, we can achieve high levels of purification and opening that will give us a deep abiding inner silence that will stay with us long after we have come home from the retreat.

Retreats provide an additional layer of practice that we can renew several times per year, resulting in accelerated progress for ourselves, and for all who are influenced by our rising enlightenment.

Retreat Basics

What are we doing when we go on an AYP retreat?

The first thing we are doing is leaving our responsibilities behind and going into an environment where there is only one priority – to systematically go deep into inner silence for the duration of the retreat, and relax and enjoy while doing it. In doing so, we will be able to cultivate a lot of purification and opening in our nervous system, and a dramatic deepening of abiding inner silence (witness) that will underlie and permeate all that we will do when we go back to normal responsibilities in our daily life.

The process that occurs on a retreat is not an intellectual learning or knowledge discipline. It is more of an unlearning that occurs as we surrender to the retreat schedule, gentle guidance of the retreat leaders, and the rise of a pervasive inner silence as we engage in our practices. The schedule will include group practice and, depending on retreat length and type, may include more than two practice sessions per day.

It is our own practices that we use when we go on retreat. If we are new to spiritual practices, the retreat will include instructions in deep meditation, spinal breathing pranayama, and basic asanas (postures), which are the core practices used on a retreat. If we are attending an advanced retreat, we may have the opportunity to receive instructions for additional practices covered in the AYP writings, such as samyama, mudras, bandhas, self-inquiry and other components of advanced practice.

Once we are on a retreat and the initial orientation and training are taken care of, then we follow the schedule for taking us gradually into deeper inner silence during the course of our stay. During this time, we may feel like we are being permeated with abiding inner silence, becoming "thick" with it, as though we are moving in it throughout the retreat. We may also experience various symptoms of purification and opening occurring at deep levels within us. We may be emotionally tearful at times, and giddy and laughing at other times. We may feel a sense of peace that surpasses all understanding. It can be anything. What we do know is that we are unloading accumulated deep stress and obstructions, and that we are going to feel much clearer as a result.

Like sitting practices at home, when we go on a retreat, it is not primarily for the experience during the retreat, though this can be and often is wonderful. But it is more for the results that we find in our life after the retreat – more stillness, peace, creativity, energy and an improved quality of life in all the things we are doing. While the results of our daily practice at home may be felt for some hours after each session, and gradually building up as a resident experience of abiding inner silence over time, the results of a retreat may be felt for months and longer. As we go on periodic retreats, we will notice a larger and longer cycle of unfoldment building underneath our daily cycle of practice. Retreats add a new dimension of progress in that way, a larger and deeper cycle of spiritual progress.

So when we say that retreats are a "fast track to freedom," we really mean it. All of the aspects of spiritual progress we have been discussing throughout the AYP writings become accelerated when we add on retreats several times each year.

Retreats are an element of practice that will take us to the next level, with a degree of support and stability on our path that will enhance our daily practice at home, and the steadily increasing joy we experience in daily living.

The Magic of Group Practice

It has been said that "there is strength in numbers."

We all know that this is true, particularly when it comes to spiritual practice. There is the famous saying attributed to Jesus:

"For where two or three are gathered in my name, there am I among them."

This does not have to be viewed from a sectarian perspective. It simply means, when people gather for a spiritual purpose, there is a multiplying effect, with the spiritual influence of the whole being much greater than the sum of the spiritual influence of the individual participants. In other words, the divine presence is amplified in the group.

In the case of an AYP retreat, we are talking about group practice for cultivating abiding inner silence, and the effect in the group is very noticeable.

While a group located in one place has a pronounced effect on all who are there, the effect of group activities can also be felt when the participants are separated by great distances. With AYP having its origin on the internet, the phenomenon of group dynamics has been felt by many around the world, whether it be in informal online communications, or the several modes of coordinated "global" group practice that have been occurring over the years. The effects of time-synchronized practice have been felt by many, even when practitioners have been spread all over the world.

On a retreat, where practitioners are gathered together in one physical place, and practicing together utilizing a specially-designed schedule, the results will be tremendously amplified. Not only tremendously amplified, but also tremendously stabilized. So the results will be much more than with individual practice, and much less likely to be accompanied by the discomforts and stability issues that can occur when individual practice at home is pressed to the limit. This is the magic of group practice.

How does this happen? Perhaps it has something to do with the resonance of consciousness at deep levels of stillness in the mind and nervous system. No one knows for sure. It can only be said that it has long been known that the inner dynamic of a group gathered for spiritual practice is far greater than the dynamic of a single individual practicing. It has to do with the coalescing of inner silence and radiating ecstatic energies that are cultivated by a group of practitioners. In this situation, the whole becomes greater than the sum of the parts, not only for the practitioners involved, but also in terms of the uplifting influence that can be felt for great distances around the location where the practices are occurring.

Such effects are lasting, and can be felt especially in places where practices have been engaged in, even long after the practitioners have gone home from the retreat. Places where group spiritual practices have been engaged in many times over many years may become "holy" places, noted for having uplifting vibrations that can be felt by many. This can be the case centuries after the original spiritual practices there have ended. Such places may become the focus of pilgrimages, which can also uplift the vibrations in that location.

So group practice can have an expansive positive influence in both time and space. For our purposes, we are looking for practical results that can benefit us in daily living, and help uplift many around the world. We can help others by helping ourselves.

Group practice is a good way to give ourselves a boost, whether it is at a weekly group meditation gathering, or on a retreat. The results can be far-reaching.

While it is possible to do a "solo retreat" from time to time and gain benefits, the biggest payoff from a retreat will come from the inner dynamics of group practice. So whenever we can get away to a retreat involving group practice, with good organization and leadership, the advice is to do it.

Short Term and Long Term Benefits

Why do retreats? Because they work for the individual, the group, and the surrounding environment, not only in the present, but with substantial residual positive effects lasting long into the future.

As the influence (initial contrast) of a retreat wears off over weeks and months after we get home, we find ourselves with a stable level of abiding inner silence beyond what we had before going on retreat. Then the next time we go on retreat, we can repeat the cycle of deep cultivation of abiding inner silence, and its integration in daily activity afterward, leading to a further increased base of inner silence. And so it goes, deeper and deeper, or higher and higher, depending on how we might view the cultivation of permanent abiding inner silence in our life.

Now let's take a closer look at the dynamics of what happens on a retreat.

Chapter 2 – Retreat Implementation

With the AYP writings being an "open source" teaching covering a full range of yoga practices, it raises some interesting possibilities. With thousands of independent practitioners undertaking these methods on their own around the world, who then is qualified to offer an AYP retreat? The answer is, anyone!

This is not the whole answer though. Obviously, there are a number of aspects that must be addressed for planning, organizing, financing and running a retreat, so some basic skills in these areas are necessary.

It can be done on several levels, from a solo retreat (one person) following a pre-planned AYP schedule, to a small retreat with 10 attendees, to a large retreat with 50 or more attendees.

All of these have the same basic requirements:

- Physical accommodations taken care of, including lodging, food, practice and meeting space, etc.

- A well-defined retreat schedule/structure to be managed by one or more retreat leaders.

- The knowledge/resources necessary to address any needs relating to attendee practices and experiences.

So, when we say anyone can organize a retreat, we mean that anyone can get the ball rolling simply by deciding to take the lead in organizing one. Then, depending on the size and scope of the retreat, one or more people can carry the planning and implementation all the way through to fruition. Within the broad community of AYP practitioners, there are ample skills and resources available to support anyone who wants to organize a retreat of any size for their area. In this way the open source nature of AYP continues to find successful application in the specialized and far-reaching discipline of implementing retreats.

If you are interested in organizing and implementing a retreat, there are several ways to go about it. Establishing contact with others involved in retreats is one place to start. It can be done on the AYP website. If you are uncertain if or how you wish to proceed, it is good to repeatedly let go of your intention to organize a retreat in stillness over weeks, months and years. If the intention is there over time like that, sooner or later, a retreat will materialize. You might be surprised how it will happen. Your intention and a willingness to act are the keys to manifesting a retreat. This is true about many things in life.

Types of Retreats

There are several common factors that have to be addressed for all retreats: comfortable accommodations, healthy food, space to walk outdoors – preferably in nature, and comfortable practice and meeting space.

Retreats come in various types and sizes, including solo, group, small, large, standard, and advanced. They also can vary in length. A week long retreat is more powerful than a weekend retreat, though a weekend will certainly be substantial in its effects.

Solo Retreat

A retreat can be as small as one person, or *solo*. This is the least complex, at least from the standpoint of logistics. The practitioner can simply go into retreat mode at home, or in a suitable environment away from home, and follow a preplanned retreat schedule in line with AYP guidelines. While the logistics may be fairly simple, sticking with the schedule and handling any unforeseen practice or experience issues may not be so simple, because there will be no one else there to support the retreat schedule or the solo practitioner. So it will take a disciplined and self-sufficient person to gain the most from a solo retreat, one who is not prone to lots of ups and downs in practice and experiences.

While a solo retreat may be easy to handle in terms of logistics, the energy of group practice will not be there, and neither will support in the form of experienced leadership to answer practice and experience questions. So a solo retreat is probably best reserved for those who have a sufficient amount of experience to carry through with such an endeavor. It is not for everyone.

Those who are considering doing a retreat for the first time will generally find a much more fulfilling experience by going to a group retreat with experienced leadership, or at least with several others present who have retreat experience who can provide peer group support. In this way, everything will be taken care of, including accommodations, management of the retreat schedule, assistance with practices (including training as may be needed), and support with the many experiences that can come up. A group retreat offers much deeper purification and opening, and longer lasting effects, due to the powerful inner dynamics of group practice.

Perhaps one of the greatest benefits of a solo retreat will be the inspiration it will give us to attend a group retreat.

Group Retreat (small)

A small group retreat is a good place to start if a larger AYP event is not scheduled and available within reasonable traveling distance. It can be undertaken in someone's house, or at a small facility suitable for such an event.

A small retreat may be less formal, where the participants know each other, or live in the same geographical area. It may be the natural outgrowth of a weekly meditation group, where the participants have gotten a taste of the transformative power of group practice and are looking for more.

Typically, a small retreat would be less than 10 people, and may or may not have an official leader. Due to the small number of people, the retreat can be run more informally, with the various duties being shared among the participants, including food, session and meeting leadership. If the experience level of most of the participants is at a similar level, the handling of Q&As in the meetings could be less leader-centric and more horizontal, with members of the group sharing their experiences accordingly. However, it is important that the retreat structure be maintained, so someone should be responsible for managing the schedule, and everyone should agree before hand to honor the structure of the retreat. Maintaining the structure is the key to a successful retreat.

Small retreats are an excellent way to gain practical experience operating in the increased inner silence that occurs whenever group practice is underway. For some, small retreats will be a great way to develop leadership skills that can lead to running larger events. We all have to start somewhere. Those who are running large retreats started out by running small ones.

Whether small retreats lead to larger ones or not, they provide strong infusions of abiding inner silence that can improve the quality of life for weeks and months after the retreat. In fact the effects of any retreat will be with us for the rest of our life, serving as a foundation in stillness that we will build on as we continue along our spiritual path.

Many prefer small retreats for the convenience and intimacy of doing group practice with a few friends for a weekend or longer. Whatever the preference may be for doing a retreat, it will be very good. The important thing is to do them regularly over the long term. Like with daily practices at home, the results are cumulative over time.

Group Retreat (large)

A large group retreat involves a more organized approach, has experienced leaders, and can accommodate many more participants, certainly more than 10, and on up into the dozens, and even hundreds.

To manage a large group retreat, more organization and planning are required, and so they are generally planned and scheduled many months in advance, and multiple leaders will be involved in the organization, financing, promotion and running of the retreat.

Even with all of this, the essential structure and running of a large retreat will be much the same as running a small one, or even a solo retreat.

The advantage of a large retreat is the greatly increased inner dynamic in stillness produced in the larger group sessions. So a large retreat has more power in stillness. And, by definition, large retreats can accommodate many more people, so they open up the opportunity for intensive group practice for those who are willing to travel to them.

Short Retreats and Long Retreats

Most of us are more likely to be going to an AYP retreat on a weekend, beginning on a Friday afternoon and ending in Sunday afternoon. This is the most common format, and the most convenient, because it can be done without taking time off from work. Typically, a weekend retreat would involve one extra practice session on Saturday morning, making it three practice sessions for the day. The group dynamic plays a major role in amplifying the effects of all the practice sessions. Perhaps surprisingly, the benefits of a short weekend retreat can be quite dramatic, giving us a boost in abiding inner silence that we can observe in contrast as we assimilate the results over weeks and months. Lots of inner silence is generated, and a lot of deep purification and opening occurs as a result.

In fact, weekend retreats can be used to build an intermediate term repeating cycle of deep penetration in stillness and grounding if several of these are attended each year. This is a cycle that can be built on top of our twice-daily meditation cycle. By combining the two, our progress on the path of purification and opening can be accelerated substantially.

A long retreat is considered to be a duration of a week or more. When we go on one of these, the number of sessions can reach two in the morning and two in the afternoon, or four each day. This would be on the middle days of the retreat, allowing one or two days at the beginning and end of the long retreat to ramp up and then back down on the number of sessions.

The main difference between a long retreat and a short one is the sustained depth of inner silence reached on a longer retreat. All of the effects are amplified considerably the longer we are in retreat mode. We go in gradually, going very deep, and we come back out gradually, retaining abiding inner silence for a much longer period when we come back out into our normal daily activity again. There is much inner silence to assimilate into activity, so a longer retreat creates a longer cycle, particularly if we repeat this kind of retreat once or twice each year.

In-between the short and long retreat, is what we could call a medium length retreat, which would be a long weekend of three or four days, usually built around a holiday weekend to minimize the amount of time taken off from regular working hours. While many may not think at first that being on a three or four day retreat during a New Years or Thanksgiving long weekend is the best idea, the benefits can be very substantial and well worth the alteration in the holiday schedule. It is a matter of what our priorities are for spiritual progress versus traditional holiday activities. So do not rule out long holiday weekends for planning and implementing a three or four day retreat. You might be surprised how many will show up. It is an economical way to cultivate more abiding inner silence while taking the least amount of time off from work.

On the other end of the scale, there is the ongoing retreat that never ends. This is the "intentional community," or "ashram" where people live and work, with the option to engage in group practice on a daily basis for as long as they are there, which could be months, years, or decades. Technically, this would not be a retreat, but it is mentioned so we will be covering the full spectrum and possibilities for group practice. Within an intentional community, there will be a distinction between regular daily practice and a retreat. In the latter, the worldly responsibilities are suspended and everyone on the retreat abides by the schedule as adapted by the retreat leaders.

Standard and Advanced Retreats

By a "standard retreat," we mean the focus of the practice sessions and training available will be for three core practices: basic Asanas, Spinal Breathing Pranayama and Deep Meditation. Every AYP retreat will include these practices performed in that order for each session. It is a lot. If additional sessions are being included in the retreat schedule, then the entire sequence is repeated with rest in-between, without getting up to leave the practice room except for bathroom breaks. Whether there are extra sessions or not, there is great purifying power in doing this routine with a group. So a standard retreat will be based on these practices, which is plenty.

For those who are doing more practices at home, these can be continued on a standard retreat as long as the retreat schedule is observed. Time for structured samyama practice will be included in the retreat schedule for those who have been doing it, but a standard retreat would not include instructions in samyama. There is only so much that can be absorbed on a standard retreat where beginners are likely to be present requiring training in the core practices. This is especially true on a short retreat. It is not the place to be adding onto the core practices.

By definition, an "advanced retreat" will first be a long retreat where there will be time for instructing in practices beyond the three core ones, plus additional time to assimilate new practices. A most likely first addition to core practices on an advanced retreat would be samyama.

While mudras, bandhas, tantric principles and other energy-related practices are introduced before samyama in the AYP writings, it can be tricky introducing these on a retreat. Even though energy related practices may not add significant time to our practice routine (mudras and bandhas can overlap with spinal breathing pranayama and meditation), they do require adjustments and acclimation that can vary widely between practitioners. It begs the question on how much instruction on energy-related practices can be accomplished on a retreat. Certainly the mechanics of energy related practices are simple enough and can be instructed. However, the implementation of them in an orderly manner may not be so straight forward with the additional purification and opening that may occur.

Individual self-pacing will usually be a much greater factor for those incorporating energy practices than for those undertaking structured samyama for the first time. This is the logic for teaching samyama first on an advanced retreat, utilizing the considerable abiding inner silence that will be present. Mudras and bandhas may also be instructed on an advanced retreat, but it is likely that they will not be stabilized for the individual practitioner until they have been taken home and utilized for some time. This is just how it is with energy practices. *Self-pacing* is the watch word.

There are other areas of practice that can be addressed in specialized ways on an advanced retreat. Standard retreats can contain particular themes, such as some kirtan (devotional singing and dancing), light self-inquiry, observing silence, or a gentle focus on various kinds of service. In advanced retreat mode, any of these, and other areas of practice, can be delved into in more depth. This is assuming that the attendees are well-established in the core practices – asanas, spinal breathing, and deep meditation.

Even so, any advanced training or additional activities should be approached in a measured way that will not dilute the effectiveness of the core practice routine. The primary purpose of an AYP retreat is to cultivate abiding inner silence. If that is taken care of, all the rest will be there.

Whatever kind of retreat we might wish to organize or attend, we will find substantial benefits. Those who are anticipating organizing and running a retreat should not be intimidated by the many variations. The most important thing is to start somewhere. The purpose of this book is to provide some inspiration and guidelines for getting started and continuing in the exciting world of retreats. With the information here and a strong desire to move ahead, you cannot go far wrong. The rewards will be well worth the effort. Whether you are an organizer, retreat leader or attendee, your participation will add much to your evolution, and to the evolution of humanity. There is great strength in numbers.

Retreat Structure and Schedule

When we say, "retreat schedule" (events in time), we are also talking about the "retreat structure" (sequence and relationship of events). These terms mean essentially the same thing, and may be used interchangeably.

By *retreat*, we mean stepping away from our normal daily routine of activities and undertaking a specific schedule designed for enhancing our spiritual progress in an accelerated way. As discussed in the previous section, this can be done in solo mode or with a group. For those who are not experienced in retreats, joining a group retreat is preferred, where everything will be taken care of and we can follow the pre-determined schedule for maximum benefit.

On a retreat there is the possibility to systematically increase the number of meditations we do in a day. This can be done by repeating our entire routine of practices a second time in the morning – adding one routine of practice for one or two days on a weekend or holiday, or on an ongoing basis if on an extended retreat. This adds a large degree of purification and deep momentum in our spiritual progress. Being free of responsibilities during the retreat is very important to accomplish the desired result. To bring our work and home responsibilities with us to a retreat can reduce the effectiveness, and can also lead to discomfort because so much is being released from inside. So it is best to let go of our responsibilities for the few days we are on retreat, and dive deep into inner silence.

If we do three routines in a day it is important to have some light activity in-between the morning and evening sessions, and in the evening as well. This is accomplished with non-strenuous walking and gentle *satsang* (group sharing). This light activity helps balance the process of releasing obstructions from the nervous system.

For two morning routines, the basic sequence of practices is asanas, pranayama, deep meditation, samyama (if doing it), rest (at least 10 minutes lying down)... and then start over. There should not be an extended delay between the first and second session, leaving the practice room only for a bathroom break as needed. In the evening, only one routine should be done. This is three full routines of practice in a day.

On an extended (advanced) retreat, the number of sessions might be increased to two in the morning and two in the evening, which would be four sessions per day, an industrial strength retreat routine for sure, and for experienced practitioners only.

Times have changed. In the past, a few decades ago, it took more sessions (sometimes even more than four per day) to achieve the same effect as can now be done with fewer sessions. In the future, it may take even fewer sessions in retreat mode to achieve good balanced cultivation of abiding inner silence. Even now, on some weekend retreats, two sessions per day has been found to be enough. It is the leaders judgment on how many sessions are to be done, calibrating to the pace a particular group can handle for best results and minimum discomfort.

World consciousness is rising, and the amount of practice necessary for good results with stability on retreats has become less. Less is more in this case. Now, and in the years and decades ahead, retreat leaders should always make adjustments in the practice schedule to suit the circumstances.

These days, three routines per day is a sufficiently ambitious schedule, especially with a group, regardless of retreat length. For purposes of this book, three routines per day is used as the baseline.

Keep in mind that group practice brings extra purifying effects in and of itself, even with our normal routine of doing two practice sessions per day. First time group retreats, where both the leaders and participants are new to retreats with the AYP practices, are best undertaken with two practice routines per day. If all goes well, a more ambitious schedule can be considered for subsequent retreats.

Do not be surprised if a lot of purification and opening occurs during a retreat, as outlined throughout this book. While advanced yoga practices are very simple, they are very powerful – especially when performed in groups. If releases become too much, then back off practices to a more stable routine immediately, and advise the retreat leaders of any difficulties. Always keep self-pacing in mind. It is one of the most important techniques in our tool kit of practices.

A typical (baseline) daily sequence of events for an AYP retreat would encompass the following:

- Rise (hygiene and light snack as needed)
- Morning Practices
- Meeting Activity (or study if solo)
- Lunch (with light social activity)

- Light Physical Activity (walking and talking with others)
- Meeting Activity (or study if solo)
- Rest
- Evening Practices
- Dinner (light social activity)
- Light Physical Activity (walking and talking with others)
- Meeting Activity (or study if solo)
- Bed

The specific timing for each of these activities and content for the meetings is provided by the retreat leaders. Sticking to a predetermined schedule is the most important rule of a retreat, and it should be adhered to as closely as possible. It is recommended not to add new practices or extensions in time of current practices while on retreat, except as may be instructed by the retreat leaders on an advanced retreat.

The beneficial effects of a retreat can be noticed for weeks or months after the retreat is over. It is like adding a longer cycle of purification and opening underneath our normal daily cycle. A retreat adds a large wave of inner silence underneath all that we do. If we attend weekend or week-long retreats two or more times per year, it can add a significant boost to our overall spiritual progress over the long term.

Planning and Running Retreats

Now we will look at the actual planning and running of retreats for several types of retreats. Setting up a retreat (even a small one) can seem like a daunting task. Clearly it is not everyone's cup of tea. Planning and running one for a larger group amounts to running a small business operation, not to mention the need for skilled leadership on the subject matter side of it, i.e., the retreat leaders.

For a medium to large retreat, no one person has to do it all. But someone has to get the ball rolling, and assistance can be brought to bear for the various parts. If we break the planning and implementation of a retreat down into its constituent parts, it becomes a much easier job to plan and implement. Good teamwork especially is the key to running medium to large retreats.

The Desire to do a Retreat

With the AYP writings being widely available around the world, it is not uncommon for there to be multiple practitioners in any particular geographical area. This is especially true in and around cities where larger populations and widespread internet access lead to more self-directed practitioners. With this occurring, it is only a matter of time before someone comes up with the desire to get together with others who are using the AYP system. This desire may lead to a meditation group that meets regularly, or there may be a desire to organize a retreat. Often a meditation group will inspire its participants to take it to the next level – a weekend retreat. Either way, a retreat begins with a desire, and if acted upon, it will lead to a gathering of practitioners. Once a retreat is in the offing, it can also lead to new practitioners who come to learn deep meditation and other AYP practices for the first time at the retreat.

The AYP online community provides support for anyone who wishes to act on their desire to form a meditation group or organize a retreat.

Connecting with Others of Like Interest

Once the desire is there, along with a willingness to act to organize a retreat, then it becomes a matter of connecting with others. There are many ways this can happen, beginning with the extended online community, leading to local networking, and also promotional activities that are specific to a particular retreat event.

How it happens is as much a function of the organizer's inclination, determination and communication skills as it is related to any particular systematic approach to promoting an event. AYP retreats have occurred as informally organized events as well as formally organized events, and as a result of both informal and formal networking and promotion.

The key to moving ahead is to develop the sense that a sufficient number of people can be attracted to a retreat event via the various networking channels available. Once there is confidence in the ability to bring together a sufficient number of attendees, then commitments can be made to facilities, a retreat date, and the retreat leaders.

Committing to Facilities and Dates

Locating and contracting for a facility is a key activity in organizing the retreat. It will also require a financial commitment, unless it is a smaller retreat being held at a private residence or donated facility.

There are many things to consider when lining up a retreat facility:

- Size, including grounds
- Options for single, double or dorm occupancy
- Meals suitable for yoga practitioners
- Adequate meeting and practice space
- Outside space for walking
- Costs

There are many facilities available within easy traveling distance from most metropolitan areas. In some cases, beautiful facilities can be found within city limits, which makes it easy for attendees to get there.

The range of lodging accommodations at any given facility is important for both individual attendee preferences (some will prefer a single room) and the cost (others will prefer a double room or dorm to save money). While a retreat is for group practice and sharing, it is also important that there be adequate privacy for attendees to process the experiences that will be occurring. So privacy in the form of single occupancy rooms at a reasonable cost will be a big plus. In general, the more flexibility a facility can provide on comfortable accommodations at a reasonable cost, the better.

The same goes for food. Some who are involved in yoga practices may be vegetarian, while others may not, so a range of dietary choices is good. For anything larger than a small gathering, food preparation is best delegated to the facility staff, and not attempted by the retreat leadership. It will be best if the retreat organizers and leaders can focus on the retreat itself, rather than on the food preparations.

An important part of lining up the facility is choosing retreat dates that will accommodate the needs of leaders and participants alike. Weekends are usually the easiest to fill for first time retreats in an area. Generally this would be from Friday afternoon (with evening arrivals acceptable) until Sunday afternoon, with departure sometime after the mid day meal. Longer retreats are also possible, and are encouraged when feasible. Longer retreats will be best attended if they contain a weekend. Even better is a long retreat encompassing a holiday weekend, so participants can attend while taking minimum time off from work.

Weekend retreats provide an easy way to cultivate a lot of abiding inner silence in a short time, which can be repeated several times per year. Longer retreats provide an opportunity for deeper penetration and cultivation of abiding inner silence, and also the opportunity for training in additional practices beyond the core practices of asanas, pranayama and deep meditation.

Judiciously choosing the time of year to schedule a retreat can also be important, depending on where you are located. For example, doing a retreat in a warmer climate during winter can attract more participants who may also be looking for a break from the cold weather. Likewise, doing a retreat in a cooler climate during summer can attract participants who may also be looking for a break from the hot weather.

Lining up Retreat Leaders

For small retreats, we may decide to take on retreat leadership ourselves. We all have to start somewhere, and there is no better place than a small gathering of spiritual friends and acquaintances. There is sufficient support in the AYP writings (including this book) and in the online community to facilitate undertaking a retreat from scratch, so to speak. If the desire is there, it can be done!

For larger retreats, utilizing an experienced leader is recommended. These are available through contact with the AYP community, and sometimes may be quite close by. If a leader must travel far, it will add a cost to the retreat, a well worthwhile expense assuming the retreat will be adequately attended.

For anyone who wishes to become a retreat leader, there is no better way than learning under the wing of an experienced leader. It is "on-the-job training." This is how we are building the ranks of experienced AYP retreat leaders. It is part of the underlying theme in the sharing of the knowledge worldwide, which we have called "peer-to-peer" transmission. Or, more romantically, "Candles lighting candles until all candles are lit."

We encourage participation in assistant leadership roles for all who may wish to become a retreat leader. Just ask, and it can be done. For those who are not inclined to lead, there are many other ways to share our emerging ecstatic bliss according to our own inclinations. All sharing is welcome.

Promoting the Retreat and Securing Sign-ups

As mentioned earlier, the networking necessary to support the filling up of a retreat may be a mixture of personal (informal) networking and a more formal program of promotion.

For small retreats that may be informally promoted, sign-ups can be handled through email and payments by whatever means the organizer and attendees agree upon. For large retreats, some sort of structured promotion will be necessary, and it will also be necessary to have a more structured approach for sign-ups, such as a "landing page" on the internet where prospective attendees can find out all of the necessary information about the retreat and sign-up, including payment with a credit or debit card, or other secure money transfer method.

The details involved in promoting and signing people up for retreats can vary widely according to who is doing it, and it is not possible to cover the many variations in approach in this book. Suffice it to say that this aspect of organizing and running a retreat is essential, and there will be as many ways to accomplish it as there are people organizing retreats. Still, there are certain principles of promotion that will apply in most cases.

In general, it will require reaching many more people with information about the retreat than the intended number of attendees in order to compensate for those who are not interested, those who are interested but can't make it to the event, and even for those who may sign up but due to personal circumstances are not able to follow through and attend. So it will be wise to cast a wide net to inform everyone who might like to attend. There are many ways to do this, both for free and for a cost. It can be done via the internet and also through the traditional media outside the internet.

Obviously, having a suitable minimum number of attendees lined up before a retreat is committed to is a good way to assure the success of the retreat. But this would be the exception rather than the rule, so promotion will be a key factor for most retreats.

A first retreat in a particular geographical region is generally the most tricky to get going. While AYP retreats have a good (and verifiable) reputation worldwide, this may have limited influence on those in a geographical area who have no direct experience from being on one. Getting a first time retreat going for the first time could therefore take some doing. The good news is that once there has been a retreat in a particular area, there will be those ready to come back for a second one, and a third one, etc. There will also be word of mouth going around an area once practitioners have gotten a taste of the deep abiding inner silence that is cultivated on retreat. So finding participants for successive retreats is usually easier to do than for first retreats. It is like that with many things in life. The first time is usually the most challenging. Once we know how, it becomes easy and fruitful for all who are involved: organizers, leaders, and participants.

The thing to do is to take the plunge and do a retreat to get the ball rolling in your area. Everyone is encouraged to do this in whatever way that is most suitable for the circumstances.

Financial Considerations

While money may be considered an anathema by many on the spiritual path, few of us can find the stability in life necessary to sustain a stable spiritual practice without at least enough of it to cover basic living expenses. Money is something that has to be given special attention when organizing and implementing a retreat, where a substantial sum may be involved for providing accommodations, food, leaders, etc., for a large group of people. It is suggested to consider the financial aspect as a vehicle for the successful implementation of the retreat.

A substantial amount of money can be involved in setting up and running even a medium-sized retreat. A key consideration in the planning stage will be structuring of the overall cost so that it can be recovered with an achievable number of paying attendees. A minimum number of attendees will be necessary for the retreat to "break-even," because some of the costs will be fixed no matter how many or how few people come, and it will take a minimum number of attendees to cover the total base cost. Base cost is determined mainly by the facility reservation cost, food, and leader travel and fees.

The pricing of the retreat per attendee will be in direct relationship to the costs and how many attendees will be necessary to bring the retreat to break-even. Pricing must also be set keeping in mind the cost of other retreats. In other words, pricing should be in line with the current market in the area where the retreat is going to occur. It should not be too high, or too low. Too high can greatly limit the number of attendees, and too low can increase the break-even number of attendees for the retreat beyond a reasonable number, perhaps even beyond the accommodations available at the retreat facility!

So be sure to do the math ahead of time, and find a reasonable balance. Remember that a retreat fee is not something that an organizer can set arbitrarily at some level above cost. Market conditions must be taken into account. In the end, no matter what we may think a retreat is worth, it will only be worth what people are willing and able to pay.

It is recommended that break-even be considered from the very beginning of the planning stage for a retreat. This will have an impact on the kind of arrangements that are entered into for facilities, and on the leaders selected, with an eye toward minimizing financial risk. All of these costs should be determined in advance, with clear agreements with the parties involved.

In addition to travel costs, leaders may charge a fee for their service, or, alternatively, may agree to a percentage of funds remaining after all costs are covered. Each retreat will be a separate business arrangement agreed upon in advance between the parties. Whoever is setting up the retreat will have the responsibility of making sure the break-even for the retreat is reasonable and attainable. If the organizer is the one putting up the front-end money, then he or she will be the one taking the financial risk.

If a retreat has a financial surplus at the end, after all agreed payments have been made, then the organizer, or whoever funded the retreat, can keep the excess, or apply it toward any other worthy cause, including helping with another retreat in the same location, or elsewhere. It is up to those who have financed and managed the retreat.

The recommendation is to do the necessary planning to make sure that no retreat will become an undue financial burden on anyone. If retreats are well-run financially, this can be a key factor in their success, and can serve as a vehicle for supporting many other retreats.

Adapting the Retreat Schedule

Every retreat is a little different. The overall duration may vary, as can the activities undertaken in-between practice sessions, which can have an effect on the degree of purification and opening occurring within all attendees on the retreat. For these reasons, the basic (baseline) retreat schedule will be adapted to suit the length and nature of the retreat. It is designed for that.

For example, a week long retreat is more likely to have additional "back-to-back" sessions scheduled during the middle days of the retreat. If a retreat is five days long, then days two, three and four may include three sessions each day. That is, two back-to-back sessions in the morning and one session in the afternoon. A weekend retreat may or may not have a back-to-back session in the morning of the second day (Saturday). It is the leader's decision.

If special activities are planned for the retreat, like an uplifting evening concert or guest speaker, then the meeting portion of the schedule may be pre-empted to a degree by that. But the practice sessions should not be pre-empted by any other activity, and sufficient rest time should not be pinched either. It is very important that the retreat schedule remain relaxed and easy.

For the same and more reasons, additional practices such as self-inquiry intensives or long asana sessions should be avoided. Besides squeezing the normal meeting times, they can also be a cause of internal energy overload for retreat participants.

The basic retreat schedule is designed to be flexible within limits, primarily to accommodate variations in practice session duration, and to permit relaxed activities and events that might be available. Beyond that, it is suggested to avoid packing the schedule with intensive activities. The results of the retreat will be best, and the longest lasting, if the schedule is kept light and easy, with primary attention on the practice sessions, supportive meetings and light social activity during meals and walks.

Teaching Practices while on Retreat

Likewise, it is suggested to be conservative about introducing too many new AYP practices during a retreat. The basic retreat will entail instructions in deep meditation, spinal breathing pranayama and a light set of asanas (postures) as needed to bring newcomers up to speed. That is a lot of instruction, especially for a weekend retreat.

Even experienced practitioners who have not been on a retreat before will have more than enough to do engaging in the group practices and multiple sessions that may be included in the retreat schedule. A weekend retreat is not the time to be adding on new AYP practices that we have not been doing at home, and certainly not practices that are outside the AYP baseline system.

For those who have been doing additional AYP practices at home, it is fine to incorporate them into the retreat sessions. Time will be made available for this by the leaders. If there is any question about this, be sure to consult with the leaders at the beginning of the retreat. The retreat schedule will be adjusted so that anyone doing samyama will have time to complete their regular routine.

There may be opportunities where the majority of attendees are experienced and have done several retreats, to include instruction in additional practices. Such retreats would be presented as "advanced" for those who wish to take on additional AYP practices, and this can be a focus of the retreat. But this would not be a typical retreat and would require special adaptation of the schedule and coverage in the meetings between practice sessions. Such a retreat would also be longer, at least one week long, to permit acclimation of the new component of practice being introduced.

For example, a retreat might be called a "Samyama Retreat" with focus on that practice, or a "Kundalini Retreat," with focus on mudras, bandhas and tantric principles, or a "Self-Inquiry Retreat," with focus on developing a practical approach the various kinds of self-inquiry, or a "Kirtan Retreat," with focus on devotional music, singing and dancing, and so on.

These kinds of specialized retreats should not be for beginning AYP practitioners. Learning deep meditation, spinal breathing pranayama and asanas, and stabilizing these in a daily routine that can be taken home, are more than enough to learn while on a first time retreat. It is unlikely that both beginners and experienced practitioners could be learning new practices at the same retreat, unless it is a long one of at least several weeks or months duration. Then there would be room to be doing several training activities at the same time, and allowing them to settle in. But not on a weekend.

Offering advanced retreats is at the option of the organizers and leaders in a particular geographical area. It is a function of a sufficient number of experienced practitioners being available for a longer retreat of this nature. It may be that practitioners would be willing to travel a long distance to attend such a retreat, so advanced retreats would have a different dynamic, involving experienced practitioners, and tending to be national or international gatherings for intensive group practice, including the addition of components of practice beyond the core practices of deep meditation, spinal breathing pranayama and asanas.

Obtaining Feedback on Retreat Results

A system of spiritual practices will only be as good as the results its users can experience through its application, and retreats are no exception in this.

During a retreat it is important for the leaders to maintain an awareness of all attendees via the meetings, the buddy system, and at other times during the day to make sure that everyone is on track for good progress with safety. Generally, attendee experiences will be deep, positive and uplifting during a retreat. On occasion there can be a few bumps, and leaders can advise on measures to smooth things out as may be necessary. With ongoing feedback, any difficulties can be addressed before they become severe.

At the end of a retreat, feedback forms should be provided to all attendees, so the quality, structure and results can be evaluated. Feedback can also be provided days, weeks and months after the retreat, online in the AYP Support Forums. Feedback plays a vital role in assisting retreat organizers and leaders in making adjustments for improvements in future retreats. It is also good to have feedback on the perceived benefits of retreats, so the organizers and leaders will know that they are on the right track in the way they are planning and implementing such events.

Geographical Considerations

By definition, retreats are going to involve some travel, even if only a short distance from home. At times, we may even be inspired to travel a very great distance to get to a retreat. The benefits can far outweigh the inconvenience.

From a planning and implementation point of view, retreats should be located within easy traveling distance from major population centers.

Ideally, retreat leaders should come from the same area as well, to hold down travel costs, which have to be built into the retreat fee. This will not always be possible, because experienced AYP retreat leaders may not be present in every geographical area of the world. Fortunately, some of the leaders that are out there are willing to travel. More importantly, they are willing to help others come up to speed to become retreat leaders in their own right.

This is much the way AYP works on the individual level with practices, where practitioners are helping other practitioners based on whatever their level of experience may be. This is leading to a steady build-up of capability in the effective application of practices and spiritual advancement across a broad community of practitioners worldwide.

A similar phenomenon is occurring with retreats, where, gradually, more and more retreats are occurring, and leaders for running them are increasing in numbers at the same time.

Anyone who is interested in learning how to organize and lead retreats is encouraged to inquire in the AYP online community. With the extensive knowledge resources we have available nowadays, and the many experienced practitioners and leaders who are involved in retreats, it is not difficult to develop the capabilities necessary to bring life-altering retreats to every corner of the globe. All it takes is an entrepreneurial spirit and determination to make a retreat happen, and it will happen.

While there has been discussion about certification of AYP teachers and retreat leaders, and it may happen at some point in time, it is not intended that this will prohibit anyone from teaching the AYP practices or leading retreats. To do otherwise would be stepping away from the practical and effective open source nature of the AYP system, which is not desired. We are much less interested in creating a hierarchy than a horizontal web of practitioners spanning the globe. Obviously, there has to be some leadership for this to happen, but it can be minimized to serve only the needs of practitioners, and not the needs of any particular organization. This is why AYP is an open resource, without any limitations for its use by anyone anywhere. So if you want to have a retreat in your area, organize one.

From a geographical point of view, as more and more retreats are occurring around the world, there should be consideration for keeping an even distribution of events in time and place, to avoid excessive overlap, which could limit the attendance at events that are too close together in time or place. For this reason, it is a good idea to advise the online AYP community of upcoming retreats, and have them listed on the worldwide retreats schedule, so multiple events can be coordinated to avoid too much overlap in location and scheduling. With such coordination, each retreat in a given geographical area and time frame can achieve maximum attendance, benefiting from retreats that have gone before, and assisting those that come after, as word of their good results spreads.

Questions, Cautions and Safety Measures

Once a retreat is underway, it will be in the hands of the leader and practitioners. For larger retreats, there may be more than one leader, but one person should be in charge, having the last word on decisions related to retreat structure, modifications and guidance for individual practitioners and the group.

The baseline retreat structure is designed to be both progressive and safe, with sufficient flexibility in it to accommodate a variety of "themes" that a leader may wish to bring to the retreat. Within the meeting periods in the retreat schedule there is room for presentations and discussions on virtually any health, personal improvement or spiritually-related topic.

However, there is very little room in the retreat schedule for the introduction of additional practices, especially any that could be regarded to be intensive.

It is common for practitioners to introduce modifications to baseline AYP practice at home, and with the tools of self-pacing there is a lot of room for experimentation. Sometimes there could be a temptation to add modifications to the practice routine on retreat. This is quite different from experimenting at home for several reasons.

First, individual experimentation is not the same as experimenting with practices when in a group, especially on a retreat, where there are many additional factors in play.

Second, the power of abiding inner silence on a retreat is greatly amplified by the dynamics of group practice, and by additional sessions that may be occurring. Additional practices outside the AYP baseline can cause accelerated purification and opening, accompanied by internal energy overload, discomfort, and destabilization of the retreat structure.

So it is recommended to stick with the predetermined retreat structure as much as possible, rather than try and invent one that will somehow produce a more favorable result. As mentioned, there is plenty of room within the baseline structure to introduce modification in presentations and discussion in the meetings. Beyond that, the risk of difficulties increases as more components are introduced. This applies to things that might be fairly mild when experimented with at home. It is a very different scenario when on retreat.

The same is true of piling on more AYP components of practice that are not yet a stable part of the home routine. For example, one may be tempted to add on a mantra enhancement for deep meditation during a retreat, or add on samyama, advanced elements of pranayama, or mudras, bandhas, etc. To do any of these things in an unstructured manner without guidance from the retreat leaders could also result in imbalance and overload on a retreat.

As already mentioned, there are particular kinds of advanced retreats where additional AYP practices can be introduced, and such retreats are specially structured for that.

Retreats are perfectly safe as long as the basic guidelines are adhered to.

Interestingly, the most common questions that come up from practitioners, whether relating to retreats or doing practices at home, are nearly always about modifying the structure of the practice routine, or about modifying the procedures of the practices themselves. With an open-source system, the temptation to tinker and add on can be very great. The AYP writings cover such possibilities from many angles, in the end saying that significant modifications to baseline practice must be the practitioner's experiment. Advanced practitioners are in the best position to undertake such modifications, and may in fact be called from within to do so. But for any practitioner, whether beginner or advanced, undertaking such modifications will include greater risk when on a retreat.

For example, if the guideline is to engage in sitting practices at home for particular lengths of time twice each day before the morning and evening meals, then the most common questions will be about variations to that. Why not have more sessions, or fewer ones? Why not longer sessions, or shorter ones? Why not doing practices after meals instead of before them? Why not practices right before bed, or in the middle of the night? These and many other questions have been answered many times in the AYP writings. In the end, it boils down to personal choice, of course. That is the nature of an open source system, and to experiment is human nature. But the truth is that it is not possible to define the causes and effects associated with an unlimited number of variations to what we have called a *baseline system of practices*. So we have said that we can help with the baseline, and the modifications will be the practitioner's experiment.

Most often the tendency will be to do more, and that can lead to internal overloading and a necessary recovery time. Those who are compelled to practice less are more likely to be on the right track, as it is our experiences that encourage us to take a wiser course in our practices. For those who want it all right now, the suggestion is to be careful and take a measured approach. That is what the baseline system is for.

Indeed, the same is true in the realm of retreats, except it is more critical due to group dynamics and the great power that is involved. It is like learning to drive a car doing a few miles an hour in a parking lot versus learning to drive on a freeway at a high speed. The retreat is the freeway.

We are pretty good now at assisting practitioners at home to get a balanced daily routine of practices going, with minimal risk for flying off the deep end. And, so far, we have done pretty well with retreats also. But in the process, we have learned that there is less room for error on a retreat due the greater depth of inner silence and greater amount of inner purification and opening that is occurring.

All of which is to say, it is best to stick with the retreat structure and guidelines from the leaders for best results.

Practitioner Questions

While it is not possible in this book to cover every question that may be asked on a retreat, we can look at some of the main ones that tend to come up:

Q1: Why do we not meditate longer per session on retreat than we do at home? Wouldn't we have even more good results if we meditated all day?

Other traditions (like Buddhist) do this on their retreats.

A1: The style of meditation we are using in AYP, including on retreats, goes very deep. While simple in its mechanics, it is very powerful in its results. For effective utilization of this style of meditation, it is important to have *cycles* alternating between the depths of inner silence we are cultivating in deep meditation and external activity which integrates the silence into our neurobiology and life.

If we were to sit for a whole day in deep meditation (or even much over 20 minutes) on retreat without resting and getting up to integrate the inner silence into our activity, we could easily end up in an inner energetic overload, with the many discomforts that go along with that. Then we are having to recover from that, and the time spent doing that (while unable to practice much at all) will delay our progress on the path.

This is why practice routines are cycled on an AYP retreat between deep inner silence and light activity.

It is also true when doing back-to-back sessions on retreat. We do our asanas, then pranayama, then deep meditation, then rest, then asanas again, pranayama again, deep meditation again, and rest again before getting up. Then we go to a meeting, a meal, and walk. All of these activities are designed to cycle inner silence from the depths within us and provide smooth integration with our daily activity, first within the retreat structure itself, and then going back out into our normal daily activity after that.

It is all about cycles going between inner and outer life. In this way, we are importing inner silence step-by-step into the fabric of our life as a permanent presence.

Q2: Why can't I do more sessions at home, more than twice a day, like we do on retreat?

A2: This is the classic question we have all asked. If extra practice sessions on retreat are good, then more extra practice sessions at home must be good too. Unfortunately, it doesn't work like that. At home, we are not in a mode of structured practice sessions and light activity that is conducive for the same kind of cultivation that occurs on a retreat. At home we have responsibilities and neither are we in the same kind of group dynamic that is the foundation of an effective retreat. Just as we keep it light and easy on a retreat, we keep it light and easy in a different way at home, where our practice is structured for being active in the world. So more practice is not always going to be the best formula for maximum spiritual progress.

In fact, the further we go along our path, we may find that *less is more*. Which is not to say we should start with that approach. There are those who say that no practice is the best practice. This is an unwise approach for those who are still developing their spiritual wings (in stillness). Once abiding inner silence has been established and pervasive around the clock, then simple devotional and/or inquiry methods may find more traction in our abiding inner silence. Until then, a balanced approach to daily practice is suggested, with the number and duration of daily practice sessions within the guidelines which have been time-tested.

The reason we have retreats is to accelerate the process within a specific program structure utilizing group practice. To increase practices at home without the necessary structure will more often than not lead to imbalances.

Q3: Can I keep mentally repeating the mantra throughout the retreat when I am not in the practice sessions?

A3: This question comes up a lot for both regular daily practice, and for retreats. The answer for both situations is the same. The mantra is a vehicle for going within utilizing a natural ability of the mind to go to stillness when a condition of mental activity without meaning (a vibration in the mind) is provided. This is what deep meditation is. Using a mantra during activity, even the reduced activity we do on a retreat will not serve the purpose of deep meditation just described, nor will it serve the purpose of providing grounding activity in-between our practice sessions. So it will be best to use the mantra when we are meditating, and engage in the prescribed activities when we are between practice sessions when we are on retreat.

Q4: What is the difference between a retreat and a vacation? Is it just as good to spend a weekend at a seaside or mountain resort, just relaxing and enjoying the scenery?

A4: There is nothing wrong with vacations. They are very good for giving us a change of pace and refreshing our point of view on life, if not the kind of deep rest found on a retreat. After a few weeks on vacation, we might be looking forward to getting back into our routine at home so we can "recover" from our very busy vacation.

A retreat is a different kind of thing. We go on a retreat to systematically dive deep within where we can find a level of rest, purification and opening that is not possible to achieve on a vacation, or even at home doing our normal daily spiritual practices. While practice at home is very good and brings solid results over time, a retreat goes much deeper, and its results will create much more contrast of abiding inner silence in our daily activity once we are back home.

We don't go on retreat for the scenery, not for the outer scenery, though is it good to have a quiet setting in nature for our retreat. A retreat is not primarily for the inner scenery either, though it can be very interesting and inspiring to observe our inner dimensions as they become more visible with the dissolving of inner obstructions deep in our subtle neurobiology. That sort of scenery is a by-product of our practice. We can enjoy it, while recognizing that our progress is the product of practice, as is the sometimes dramatic inner scenery that might come along with it.

Q5: Is it alright to arrive a day late to a retreat, or leave early if necessary?

A5: We all will do what we must in the course of our life. Attending part of a retreat may be better than not coming at all, but the results will be less than optimal. It can also create some bumps on the flow of group consciousness on the retreat. So if you have schedule requirements that would have you arriving late or leaving early, it will be best to check with the retreat leaders beforehand. Ideally, everyone should be there for the duration for best results.

In case of an emergency, departing a retreat for healthcare or to attend to other urgent personal needs is certainly all right. In such cases, your buddy and/or the retreat leaders should be notified.

Q6: Is it all right to bring my spouse on retreat? How about bringing the children?

A6: It is wonderful to bring your spouse on a retreat. Then you will both be in deep abiding inner silence together, which can increase your mutual understanding about what is at stake with practices, and also accelerate progress when you bring the dynamic of your "group of two" home again into daily practice in your normal life.

If you do come as a couple and sharing a room is not too much distraction, then this is fine. If single occupancy rooms are available, you might find the extra privacy helpful for individual processing during the retreat. It can be done either way. One of the features of a retreat is balancing group practice and interactions with individual inner processing. This is why single occupancy rooms can offer some advantage, though it is certainly not mandatory, as discussed previously in this chapter.

While bringing small children on a retreat is not impossible (assuming adequate child care has been arranged), it is generally not recommended. This is particularly true of a small retreat where space will be limited and the presence of small children may disturb other practitioners. Small children should not be brought into practice sessions or meetings, and that will limit the time for parents to be with their children. So arrangements for child care will be necessary. While small children are angelic and can be uplifting, they can also disrupt the flow of a retreat. So it may be best to arrange care for them at home while on retreat. If leaving the children is not an easy option, it may make sense for a couple to take turns with each one going on retreat while the other stays home with the children. This is the more common solution for couples with children, and it can work out fine. Where there is the will, there is a way.

Once our children reach an age where they are ready for adult practice, and are interested in pursuing it for themselves, then it will be very good to bring them on a retreat. This would generally be at about 18 years old, though they can be ready when younger in some cases. A parent can sense what is best, in stillness.

Q7: Why am I laughing so much on retreat?

A7: The nature of inner silence is "pure bliss consciousness." It is also our true nature. There is no greater evidence of the bliss component than what we will often experience on a retreat – bliss that permeates us through and through. The most visible symptom of bliss is laughter. It can travel in waves through a group of participants on retreat.

We may have this going on when we get home also. It can be misinterpreted to mean we do not care anymore, particularly when difficulties are occurring around us, and we are able to smile as our bliss radiates through whatever dark moods others may be in, or even our own moods! But it is not an uncaring we experience as we live increasingly in bliss. On the contrary, our compassion becomes greatly elevated and we are much more inclined to act for the betterment of others. Their pain becomes our pain, even as we are permeated with the bliss of surging abiding inner silence. It is one of the paradoxes of human spiritual transformation.

Q8: Why am I having strong negative emotions?

A8: When purifying energy moves within us and passes through obstructions, there can be some *friction*, leading to some discomfort. Generally, this will be mild and short-lived, assuming we are following the program structure and any additional instructions we may receive from the leaders on our retreat.

Many find that they have less of a tendency to have negative emotions on a retreat than they might have at home. It is another one of those paradoxical things.

The quantity of inner silence that is cultivated on a retreat is so huge, and its quality so permeating, that negative emotions tend to be washed over with pure bliss. Even if there is some surface angst, we might ask, "Negativity? What negativity?" In the deep witness quality of abiding inner silence we can observe it from a distance, even if there is some negativity in what might have been considered an intimate part of us before. Nevertheless, sometimes we can find ourselves in a bit of a funk on retreat. It is not unheard of, one of the many possible symptoms of purification and opening. If it gets to be excessive, that is the time for self-pacing, extra grounding and rest. The symptoms will pass as our inner pathways are gently opened.

Q9: Sometimes I have inspired thoughts and revelations during practices on retreat, but then I forget them almost right away. Should I be taking notes during the sessions?

A9: Definitely do not be taking notes during your sessions on retreat, or when practicing at home either. Thoughts that come up during deep meditation, including the thought, "This is a revelation!" are symptoms of purification occurring, and should not be analyzed while we are practicing. When we notice we are off the mantra, we just easily come back to it at whatever level of clarity or fuzziness we find ourselves in the mind. This is how we go progressively deeper into more silent levels in our neurobiology, cultivating abiding inner silence into our nature.

When we are out of our session, we will have access to the creativity that abiding inner silence brings into all aspects of our life. This is certainly true when we are at home and engaged in our daily life. On retreat, it is different. We should regard all time on retreat as though we are in a long practice session, and refrain from making important decisions, even when between practice sessions. It is fine to be

Fast Track to Freedom – 55

OK to take notes in between sessions

making a few notes when between practice sessions on retreat, but it is suggested holding off on making decisions until back home with feet firmly on the ground. Those revelations may not look the same when viewed in the light of practical daily living.

There is the old story about the practitioner who was on retreat, having very deep meditations. He kept getting a sense of something important coming from within that had the vibration of a great revelation. It was blissful and huge, like a giant white cloud welling up within him. He knew this was momentous, and was inspired to capture its import, which he felt could change his life.

Finally, as the experience came up again during a session, he hung on to it, managing to stay with it until it slowly came into focus in the eye of his cognitive mind. And there it came, getting clearer and clearer. What was this great revelation he was about to grasp that would change his life forever?

Then he cognized it: "Marshmallow..."

Yes, this was the profound revelation that came to our meditating friend while he was on retreat.

It goes to show that thoughts during meditation should not be evaluated for their content. This applies especially when on retreat, where obstructions are being dissolved deep within us and the content of thoughts coming up will not have any meaningful relationship to our life. They are just a byproduct of purification and opening, and we will do best by favoring the mantra whenever we find that we are off it. When on a retreat, we will also do best to avoid making important decisions. The "marshmallow effect" can happen at any time during a retreat. It is all for the good.

Q10: Should I expect visions or clairvoyance on retreat?

A10: In spiritual practice it is usually not a good idea to cultivate too many expectations about anything. This is tricky because, obviously, we are engaged in practices for a reason. The same is true about going to a retreat. We have our reasons. We have expectations about the cause and effect of the things we do. Whatever we may be expecting, the truth is that the result of our practice will be fewer expectations as we become the underlying reality behind anything we may have been expecting: the root cause of all external manifestation – abiding inner silence.

So will we experience visions and clairvoyance on a retreat? Maybe. Maybe not. There will be symptoms of purification and opening for sure. What they will be exactly will depend on the unique matrix of obstructions being dissolved within us. The real fruit of the retreat will be the natural emergence of non-attachment to whatever the symptoms may be.

The best attitude we can have on a retreat is to go and have a good time, enjoy the good company, stay on the schedule as best we can, and take whatever happens in stride. Always favor the practice over the experience.

Q11: Why do we walk on retreat? Can I jog like I do at home?

A11: Walking, preferably with someone, on a retreat is to help ground and stabilize the deep inner silence we are cultivating during the practice sessions. It is done after the midday and evening meal. It is not primarily for exercise that we do it. It is for integrating inner silence into our neurobiology, which permeates every cell within us.

Asanas serve a similar purpose, with less grounding effect. Asanas open up our inner neurobiology in preparation for spinal breathing pranayama, deep meditation, and other practices we may have in our routine. So asanas are not mainly for grounding, but they do facilitate the flow within us, and help balance it.

Physical exercise beyond light walking and asanas is not recommended on a retreat. Intensive exercise breaks down the muscles and other components of the physiology so they can grow back stronger.

When we are on retreat, we are engaging in a different kind of intensive exercise, which is expanding our inner neurobiology. As we do the light physical activities on retreat, we are facilitating the strengthening of our subtle neurobiology as a vehicle for inner silence and the divine flow. This requires some acclimation, both on the retreat and after we get home, and that is the main priority of a retreat.

Adding strenuous physical activity while on retreat can be disruptive to the inner processes that are already occurring. External exercise is best done when we are in the external world. While on retreat, we will be best served by focusing on our internal exercise.

Q12: Do I have to eat vegetarian on retreat, even if I don't at home?

A12: No, it is not a requirement. The most important thing on a retreat is that we are comfortable with the routine so we can gain the most from our presence there.

AYP retreat meals are planned to accommodate a range of diet preferences. You may not find a juicy steak on the menu, but fish and foul should be readily available, along with vegetarian fare. Everyone's diet requirements are a bit different, and retreat planning will take this into account.

We may find that, as we are meditating over months and years, our preferences may shift toward a more light and nutritious diet. On a retreat, this can happen also. But the diet we are eating is not a prerequisite for anything else we are doing on a retreat. As we are cultivating abiding inner silence, we find that diet becomes more effect than cause on our path. Of course, a healthier diet can yield better health. With meditation alone, we can look forward to that. Being on a retreat can accelerate our migration toward more healthy living in all ways.

Q13: I felt really tired on my last retreat. All I wanted to do was sleep. Must I fight to stay on the schedule if my body is crying to do nothing but sleep?

A13: No, you don't. If you find yourself sleeping through most of the practice sessions, that is okay. If you are too tired to get to the practice sessions, or to meetings or meals, it is alright to stay in your bed in your room. That would be an extreme case, but if that is what our nervous system needs, it is what we should do. <u>Make sure to let your buddy and the retreat leaders know.</u>

Being on a retreat is to be in an environment that is permeated with abiding inner silence, whether we are meditating with the group or not. Of course, it is best to be in the group sessions if we can be, but if our body needs to take extra deep rest that is being caused by the retreat environment, then we should take it. A lot of purification and opening will be occurring regardless, and we will feel much better afterward.

A retreat is for our purification and opening, and sometimes it can take an unusual form. We can honor that as long as we are safe and comfortable.

Q14: I felt giddy on the way home from the retreat, and for a few days after. Why is that, and will it continue at home and at work?

A14: This is an overflow of bliss consciousness after the retreat, and is very normal. As we become active in the world again, our abiding inner silence (pure bliss consciousness) gradually permeates everything we do in life. Over time, we will notice a fading of giddiness, and the rise of a sense that our life is becoming an ongoing experience of *stillness in action*.

Certainly our sense of humor will not go, and we will still notice that giddy blissful outpouring occurring at times. But it will be more balanced in relation to everything else we are doing. Our effectiveness in life will improve, not get lost in a sea of laughter, though we might wonder about that at times, when waves of bliss are pouring through.

When we are ready to take our abiding inner silence a level higher, we can go on another retreat. Then we might have another surge of giddiness too. But let's be mindful not to be expecting much other than our gradual liberation. Step-by-step...

Cautions and Safety Measures

With the retreat schedule we use, adapted by the leaders for the duration and kind of retreat, there will be little that can go wrong. However, everyone is a bit different in the way they might experience purification and opening, so there may be times where the emotions or some mental or physical sensations may become noticeable to the point of distraction from staying with the retreat schedule. This is not the usual scenario, but it can happen. When such symptoms occur, it is suggested to advise the retreat leaders of anything out of the ordinary causing excessive distraction or concern. If any symptoms become extreme to the point where there is fear or a desire to leave the retreat, then the leaders should be advised immediately, no matter what time of the day or night such feelings may be experienced.

For any retreat with more then 5-10 people, it is recommended to set up a buddy system at the beginning, where practitioners are paired off, with the responsibility to keep an eye on each other. This helps everyone keep on the schedule, including practice sessions, meetings, meals, walking and talking, etc. If there should be any difficulty or inability to follow the schedule, the buddy can be notified, who can then let the retreat leaders know, as appropriate.

As discussed earlier, there will be times when extra rest may be necessary, sometimes to the point where a meeting or meal may be missed. This is okay, as long as a buddy and the retreat leaders are notified. The purpose of the retreat is deep rest, accumulating at successively deeper levels as the retreat progresses. Sometimes, this can lead to a need for a lot of sleep, and that is to be honored.

In the event of symptoms of excessive purification, it is important for the practitioner to self-pace accordingly. If there is any doubt about what to do, then the retreat leaders should be consulted. Their job is to manage the structure of the retreat in such a way that the all participants gain the most benefit with the least discomfort. If someone is experiencing too much discomfort, the leader may advise the practitioner to stop after one session in the two session sitting. Or perhaps even shorten the components of practice within a session. In an extreme case, the leaders may suggest skipping a session and resting in bed or walking instead. This is rare, but it can happen. As we know, "self-pacing" is a key part of applying the AYP system of practices, and this applies on a retreat also.

In fact, retreat leaders themselves can begin to overload at times, and it is obviously important for them to self-pace also. This might mean not participating in all practice sessions. Leading meetings and constantly interacting with practitioners is also deep spiritual practice, so leaders may at times choose to separate themselves from the group when not directly engaged in activities where their presence is required. This is normal. Leaders should not feel that they have to be 100% engaged twenty-four hours per day for the duration of a retreat.

With good planning, experienced leadership, and the buddy system, any issues that might come up can be managed with a positive outcome for everyone on the retreat.

A Typical Day on a Retreat

So far, we have covered the basics of planning and implementing a retreat. The information is for leaders, practitioners, and also for those who would like to become leaders.

If you are new to all of this, you may be wondering what it is like being on an AYP retreat. Each will have its own flavor, depending on the leaders and the makeup of the group. But all retreats have one thing in common – the cultivation of a lot of abiding inner silence. The results of that have been discussed already, and there will be further discussion through the course of the rest of this book. It is results in our life we are looking for, after all.

To give a better idea about what an AYP retreat might feel like while in progress, consider the following. Of course, everyone is different in how purification and opening occurs, so this particular scenario should be regarded as typical:

Today is Saturday. You wake up about 7:00am, remembering the evening before, which was the first night of the retreat. After arriving on Friday in the mid afternoon and meditating in your room, you mingled a bit with other attendees for the first time at dinner. The evening meeting was busy, with the leaders giving a warm and good-humored welcome, determining who needed training, and laying out the schedule for the weekend. They helped all of the retreat participants pair up with a "buddy" to assure everyone would be accounted for throughout the retreat. At the end of the meeting, instructions were provided for deep meditation, spinal breathing pranayama and a short set of asanas. You hung around for that, since you have only been doing deep meditation for a few months before the retreat. Bedtime was at around 10:00pm.

So now you are awake on Saturday morning. After a shower, getting your comfy meditation clothes on, and a light snack, you decide to do asanas in your room before heading to the hall for pranayama and meditation. You could have gotten up earlier for a bigger breakfast, but you were advised that eating much before morning practices is not recommended.

Asanas are a clunky affair, as you are fairly new to them, but you get through the routine without any strain, as instructed. The sheet with diagrams of the 12 or so postures handed out the night before is helpful. The asanas take about 15 minutes, and then you are off to the meditation hall with pillow and blanket under your arm, arriving about 7:45am.

As you quietly enter the meditation hall, you notice a few people finishing up asanas there, including your buddy, who acknowledges you with a nod. There are several people sitting against the wall doing pranayama. A few more are sitting in the middle of the room leaning against "back jacks" and a few on cushions without back support. Two senior citizens are sitting in easy chairs. You think how nice it is to be comfortable like that, and you find a spot against the wall where there is already a pillow to sit on, so you use yours for back support.

By the time you finish pranayama, everyone is in place for an 8:00am start of meditation – right on schedule. This is your first time on a retreat or in a large group, so you are not quite sure what to expect. After about 5 minutes of meditation, you realize you are deep into stillness, which is surprising since you are not yet acclimated to the group setting. It is as though the bottom fell out of all your expectations and here you are in stillness. Your whole inner world is on a cloud of palpable silence. About 10 minutes into the meditation, you check your watch, and you cannot help but notice the group. A few heads are drooping in a nodding off fashion, a few bodies are wiggling, but most are silent and still. You close your eyes and back in you go, picking up the mantra in the fluffy cloud of stillness you have become inside.

After 20 minutes, you lie down to relax as instructed. You seem to be floating. Several in the group are still sitting, presumably doing samyama. One fellow is panting a lot and moving in sudden jerks. After another 10 minutes, everyone is lying down. You drift off.

The next thing you know you become aware of someone doing asanas a few feet away. It is the second session, which the leaders said would be happening this morning. So you spread your blanket and do your asanas for the second time. Then back into pranayama, and at 9:00am, everyone is meditating again. By the time you lay down at the end of the second session, the blissful silence is so thick that you feel you could cut it with a knife. As you lie on your blanket, you suddenly burst out laughing at the thought of slicing the silence into pieces with your hand and smooshing it back together like clay. Then others are laughing. Who let them in on the joke? Waves of bliss are undulating over the group. Is group practice always like this?

By the time 10:00am rolls around, everyone is getting up and filtering out of the hall in a quiet fashion. Blankets and pillows are left behind. They will come in handy for upcoming meetings and practice sessions.

The morning meeting is scheduled for 11:00am, so there is some time to relax in the room, read a little, eat that piece of fruit saved from dinner last night, but no heavy mental or physical activity. By now you don't feel like it anyway. Let the world go its way. <u>You are on vacation in deep inner silence.</u> Everywhere you look there seems to be a glow. Somehow it seems normal, but you are still getting used to it. You are moving slowly and enjoying it immensely. It is a kind of intoxication, but one of seeming great clarity. Each thought that comes seems profound. Should you be writing all this down? Never mind.

After a while, you get dressed, put on your walking shoes and go to the 11:00am meeting. Your buddy is coming out at the same time you are, and that is good. By the time you get to the meeting, the billowing silence inside seems to be moving up and out through the top of your head. It is a bit disconcerting to find that the walking and the stillness are one and the same thing. And you feel some emotions surging, like you could cry at any moment. You are not used to this.

Chairs are available for the meeting, and you are grateful for that. Some still opt for the floor. The leaders ask how everyone is doing, and a wave of soft laughter travels across the room. You laugh too, and your emotions seem to settle into silence. You are not alone in this unfamiliar expanded state of consciousness. Quite to the contrary. You feel a deepening kinship with these people you only met the night before. It seems so long ago.

"Very good then. Any questions on practice or experience?"

You ask about the experience of energy moving and the strong emotions causing some discomfort, and the leaders advise that this is normal, and should settle in by the time you have lunch and do some walking afterward. There are some other questions on various experiences others are having, and it goes around, with interesting and sometimes very funny stories being shared. There is a closeness in the group that is difficult to describe, and now you are getting weepy about that. There is a sensation that this is a homecoming, and you feel relief to the point of tears.

After more questions and answers, it is 12:00 and everyone is off to lunch. Insightful sharing happens there over good food. Then it is time to walk for about 30 minutes, so the group breaks up into twos and threes and fives and off you go, enjoying the great outdoors and grounding the cosmic stillness that is in and all around you. At the same time there is talking with your walk-mates. You keep it light and easy, not attaching too much to anything. And you are feeling better, flowing in stillness with less obstruction. The emotional tension that was coming up before is gone, perhaps gone out through your feet into the ground. The walking definitely seems to have helped. You were told this is the best way to navigate a retreat. Just relaxing and following the schedule. Very easy. Let it happen. Inner silence is doing everything.

After another stop by the room, lying down for a while, you go to the afternoon meeting at 2:00pm. It has a more grounded tone than the morning meeting, and the topics discussed add confirmation to much that has been happening with practices and experiences both at home and on the retreat. The meeting ends at 3:30, and you take a break in your room again. Meditation starts at 4:30pm in the hall, so you go there at 4:00 and do your asanas and pranayama.

There is only one session on Saturday afternoon, and dinner is at 6:00pm. All goes well with the session. After dinner, there is another walk for about 30 minutes. You are still swimming in silence, but somehow more grounded too.

The evening meeting starts at 7:30. There is more discussion and camaraderie, and also a spiritual video. It is perceived as a blurry dance in your awareness, but you enjoy it anyway. What's not to enjoy? The evening meeting is as much social as business – a time to just be with the group for a few questions, some inspiring talk and light entertainment. The entire group is sailing along in abiding inner silence. No one seems to be exempt. At times the meeting is ruled by hilarious laughter. You look forward to taking this home into your busy life. What a merging it will be.

The Saturday evening meeting is over, and you are back in your room by 10:00pm. You do a little reading, and then turn off the light and drift off into a deep conscious sleep.

On Sunday there is one session in the morning at 8:00am, a meeting at 11:00, and lunch at 12:00. Then everyone is beginning to leave. Lots of hugs and good wishes expressed to meet up at the next retreat. The retreat is complete, and the expansive inner silence that has been cultivated is on its way out into the world, where it is much needed.

This description of a typical day on a retreat is not to project an exact scenario for everyone, but only to give a general idea of what it is like. The schedule times could be different, depending on leader decisions on applying the baseline schedule. There is room for adapting the schedule as may be necessary to accommodate a variety of objectives and situations. At the same time, there is a baseline structure that will lead to the best results, and the typical day scenario is offered to give a flavor for that.

The experience of our participant has not been overstated. In fact, some who have attended AYP retreats might consider the typical day description to be understated. Each will have their own experience. You will have to attend a retreat to find out what it is for you. Based on feedback from the many who have attended these events, you are not likely to be disappointed.

Transitioning Back to Normal Daily Activity

A retreat is a journey into stillness – deep abiding inner silence. We have been reviewing the kinds of experiences that can occur as this journey progresses, and will continue to do so in the next chapter. The retreat schedule is designed to accommodate all of the inner dynamics that occur during a retreat. The schedule is also designed to bring us back out in a way that facilities a smooth transition back to normal daily activity.

When we do our twice-daily practice routines at home involving asanas, spinal breathing pranayama, deep meditation and additional elements of practice, we always come out slowly with ample rest at the end of our session. This smoothes the transition back to normal activity, avoiding unwanted discomfort from any residual inner purification and opening that has been occurring during our practice. The rest period at the end of our sessions is as important as the practice itself.

Likewise, when the retreat is winding down, the leaders will guide us gently through a routine that comes back to normal daily practice at the end, with plenty of rest leading to a smooth transition as we leave the retreat.

Nevertheless, we are bound to feel pretty high as we go back out into the world, infused with pure bliss consciousness. It is common to feel a bit "blissed out" for the first few days after a retreat. It is good to honor that with some extra rest, and not plunge into intense activity immediately upon arriving home. Better to take it easy for a few days and ease back into full-fledged activity. We may not always have a choice in this. We may be coming home on a Sunday, and have to go back to our busy job on Monday. It will not be the end of the world, but it could be a little jarring. If we have a choice, we should take it easy for a day or two before fully engaging in worldly life again. A gradual phase-in will be better than suddenly jumping back in.

There is an effect from the retreat itself that can push us into too much activity too soon. Abiding inner silence has the quality of boundless energy and creativity, and sometimes coming off a retreat, we may be inspired to tackle too many things at once. This can lead to a bit of overdoing, and some letdown. Keep in mind that the full positive effects of having abiding inner silence in our life are found by striking a balance between practices (in this case coming off a retreat) and integrating the effects of that with our daily activity. Once we have done so with a smooth transition back into activity, we will find that our actions in the world are manifesting within the abiding inner silence we have been cultivating. We call this the rise of "stillness in action." It is a very dynamic and progressive way of living, even as we are abiding in stillness all the while. It is one of the paradoxes of spiritual life.

There is a parallel between daily practice and retreats. With one we are doing a short cycle of going deep, resting, and then integrating back in daily activity. With the other, we are doing a long cycle of going very deep, resting, and integrating back into a much longer period of activity infused with pure bliss consciousness. This is the advantage of doing retreats. They accelerate our progress toward living a fuller and happier life over the long term by adding a long cycle of practice on top of our short cycle of daily practice.

Let's now delve into more detail on what is happening within us on a retreat, beginning with a summary of the core practices we use: deep meditation, spinal breathing pranayama and asanas.

Chapter 3 – The Inner Dynamics

We have reviewed the basics of why we should consider going on retreats, as well as the baseline structure, planning and implementation of them, and what happens experientially while we are there. Now we would like to go into more detail on the inner dynamics, the causes and effects that are at work while we are on retreat. It is a profound change that is happening within as we step up our practice in the company of others who have the same interest in advancing their evolution.

What happens is complex both in terms of our practices and the experiences they produce, encompassing every cell and atom within us as each and every part of us is bathed in inner silence likely more so than we have experienced at any time in our life. Yet, the signs and symptoms are observable and can be categorized. And, fortunately, the practices themselves are very simple. All we have to do is bring our desire to the table, and a willingness to act according to the established and time-tested guidelines. So what is it that we are doing that brings about this rarified atmosphere of inner silence and divine outpouring that occurs on a retreat?

Reviewing the Core Practices

Aside from the retreat structure and group dynamics, we have mentioned three practices as being the core of what we are using when we go on an AYP retreat – <u>deep meditation, spinal breathing pranayama, and asanas (postures)</u>. Let's review them, keeping in mind that complete instructions on these and many complementary practices can be found throughout the AYP online writings and books. What is given here is for introductory purposes only, and not intended to be a complete instruction.

Deep Meditation

Most certainly at the center of the AYP approach to spiritual practice is deep meditation with a mantra. The reason for this is because it is the simplest, most direct, and most powerful means for cultivating abiding inner silence, the essential quality that exists within us all. This quality has been given a multitude of names throughout human history, all meaning the same thing – inner silence, emptiness, void, pure bliss consciousness, the witness, sat-chit-ananda, Tao, the peace that surpasses all understanding, and so on. This eternal presence within us has often been personified, forming the root of the many faiths found in the religions. It is our essential nature, and is directly accessible with an effective technique. It is beyond the trappings of religion, while at the same time compatible with the truth found in every religion. It is also non-religious, in the sense that the technique of deep meditation works whether we are religious or not. It is a process of deep neurobiological awakening, and no one is excluded from doing that.

Deep meditation is a simple mental technique that enables us to cultivate abiding inner silence and all that it leads to, which in AYP we have called *human spiritual transformation*. It means simply endless peace, creativity and happiness in every day life. We all have that potential inherent within us.

So what is this practice? It is sitting comfortably with eyes closed for 20 minutes twice each day, before the morning and evening meal, and favoring the inner thought of the mantra. Using a chair with back support is all right – the less distraction in our chosen seat the better, as long as we are in a relatively upright position.

The mantra we use is I AM (as pronounced in English), which also can be spelled AYAM. It is the sound we favor in the mind, not any particular meaning. During our sittings, we will find our attention being occupied by thoughts feelings and sensations. Each time we notice we have become absorbed in thoughts, feelings or sensations we just easily favor a repetition of the inner sound of the mantra. It can be clear, fuzzy, or anywhere in-between. We just favor it wherever it is, whenever we realize we are not. The repetition of the mantra can change, as can how it is perceived – fast, slow, clear, fuzzy. All of these are correct. We don't try to make the mantra fast or slow, clear of fuzzy. Neither do we try to push out other thoughts or sensations that come up. They may be there at the same time we are thinking the mantra. This is normal. So we do this easy procedure for 20 minutes, and then take a few minutes to rest before we get up and go about our daily business. That is all there is to it.

On retreat, we take a much longer rest to integrate the deep inner silence we are cultivating.

What we accomplish with this practice is to bring the mind, and corresponding neurobiological activity, repeatedly to very quiet levels of functioning. Mind and body are intimately connected, and go to stillness together with this technique. We may notice our breathing becoming very faint during deep meditation. This is normal.

Deep meditation is much different than simply sitting quietly for 20 minutes, and also much different than trying to empty the mind or favoring "stillness" for 20 minutes. The difference is that deep meditation with mantra like this takes advantage of a natural ability that the mind has to go to stillness by itself. All we are doing with the mantra is setting up a condition where this can happen naturally and repeatedly for the time we are sitting. It is a progressive method, not passive, and also very powerful as many have attested.

In fact, too much deep meditation can bring us into a state of overdoing with our inner purification and opening. This is why we place a lot of emphasis on "self-pacing," "grounding" and additional measures as may be needed for a smooth awakening of abiding inner silence within us. While this quality in us is stillness in the ultimate sense, it is also the most dynamic aspect of our nature.

So when we are home, we practice this twice each day and go out and stabilize the inner silence we are cultivating in normal daily activity. The result is more progress and joy in daily activity, and more abiding inner silence being stabilized in our life and in our surroundings. And on retreat, we are going much deeper than we do at home, so when we come back out into our life again, we will be infused with a vast amount of abiding inner silence, which we then can enjoy and stabilize in our daily life over weeks and months.

Spinal Breathing Pranayama

Breathing techniques have played a key role in spiritual practice for thousands of years, as has combining an easy placing of attention in the body along with the breath. Spinal breathing pranayama in various forms has been around for a long time. In AYP, we use a very simple version, which has been found to be very effective for opening up the subtle neurobiology prior to deep meditation. So this practice is done right before deep meditation, typically for 5-10 minutes. We sit comfortably with eyes closed, just as we do for meditation.

Spinal breathing pranayama is gentle deep breathing, while tracing the "spinal nerve" with our attention between the perineum (root) and the point between the eyebrows (brow). In-between those two locations, we follow an imaginary tiny tube up through the center of the body, or within the spine if this is easier. It is not so important to trace an exact path as it is to end up at the brow at the end of inhalation and at the root at the end of exhalation. Later on, the path of the spinal nerve will become more clear as an ecstatic conductivity arises in the body. Then it may be a tiny thread of ecstatic sensitivity going between the root and brow. Later on, this tiny thread can become quite large and ecstatic, encompassing the entire body, and beyond. When we are doing spinal breathing pranayama, we always easily favor the center in a similar way we do the mantra in deep meditation. When we notice that our attention during spinal breathing has gone off somewhere physically or mentally, we just easily bring our attention back to whatever level of awareness we have had, clear or fuzzy, tracing between root and brow as is comfortable.

When we have completed our 5-10 minute spinal breathing session, we take it easy for a minute or two and then begin our deep meditation session.

For those who are new to these practices when coming on a retreat, it will be a lot of learning in a short time. Instead of jumping into spinal breathing pranayama right after learning deep meditation, the retreat leaders may suggest beginning with an easy form of pranayama called "alternate nostril breathing" before our meditation instead of starting off with spinal breathing right away.

Alternate nostril breathing is done by breathing normally while using the thumb and index finger of one hand to close alternate nostrils – breathing out and then in through one nostril, then switching to the other nostril to breath out and in, and then repeating back and forth for the 5-10 minutes of our pranayama session before deep meditation. When we are ready to begin practicing spinal breathing pranayama, then the alternate nostril breathing can be replaced with that. Both kinds of pranayama should not be used in sequence in the routine, as this could lead to overdoing in pranayama.

The effects of pranayama are a relaxing and opening of the subtle neurobiology, creating a more conducive environment for deep meditation and the rise of abiding inner silence. So pranayama is a preparation for meditation. So too are asanas (postures) a preparation for pranayama and meditation.

Asanas (postures)

Yoga postures are wildly popular around the world today, and for good reason. Beyond physical conditioning and relaxation, they provide an effective foundation for the performance of progressively deeper yoga practices after the routine of postures is complete, a fact that is often overlooked by many who are drawn to yoga postures.

This is how postures are utilized in AYP, including on retreat, as a preparation for pranayama and deep meditation. Each of the core practices we are discussing here takes our inner neurobiology toward progressively deeper levels of purification and opening. Postures do it on the physical level. Pranayama does it on the more subtle level of the breath, opening up our inner neurobiology, using postures as a springboard for that. And deep meditation takes us deeper still, beyond the subtle neurobiology into the realm of pure bliss consciousness, using the mind as the medium and the mantra as the vehicle.

So this is the order we do the three categories of practice in a session – <u>asanas</u>, <u>pranayama</u> <u>and meditation</u>. Once we have completed a session, we rest. If we are home, the rest period can be a few minutes, or whatever we need to complete the purification process we have been cultivating in our session. When we are on a retreat, the rest period can be longer, 10-15 minutes or more. Resting lying down is how we do it when on retreat. And lying down is also good when we are at home, if possible.

Because of the full scope of practices we have in a typical AYP practice session, with asanas, pranayama and meditation, we do not do asanas to the extent or rigor found in a typical yoga studio setting, where postures are usually a stand-alone practice. If asanas were to be undertaken to this extent, for 30 minutes, an hour or more, this would throw the overall routine out of balance, and could lead to symptoms of overload in purification and opening.

Instead, a typical asana routine included at the beginning of an AYP practice session is 10-15 minutes. That is all that is necessary to prepare the body/mind for pranayama and deep meditation. And this is done before each session, so it is twice per day at home, and can be three or four times per day in an extended retreat mode. So the time in postures can add up, but we always do it as a preparation (warm-up) for pranayama and deep meditation.

Those who are avid asana practitioners, going to the yoga studio several times per week, may continue to do that. But it should not come as a surprise when more purification is found to be going on, maybe with discomfort, when doing an AYP routine at home. On retreat, if longer asana routines are undertaken, the effect can be a dramatic overdoing, and a word to the wise should be sufficient on that. A retreat is not the right place to be experimenting with excessive practices of any kind. An hour of asanas in a yoga studio near home is not the same as an hour of asanas on an AYP retreat. It is nearly always better to abide by the schedule and the retreat leader's suggestions.

Regarding what postures to do in a 10-15 minute asana routine, this is covered in the AYP writings, where an "Asana Starter Kit" is provided with about a dozen postures, with several variations also available to cover both a shorter abbreviated session and also an enhanced routine for more experienced practitioners. In any of these asana routines, the

Fast Track to Freedom – 83

practice time is designed to be less then 15 minutes, and as preparation for pranayama and deep meditation.

When beginners come to an AYP retreat, deep meditation, pranayama and asanas will be taught, so the full benefit of the retreat can be experienced. For those who are accustomed to doing long asana sessions, a toning down will be necessary, to provide a balance for introducing pranayama and deep meditation. The goal is a smooth and progressive experience for all, with lots of abiding inner silence being cultivated, which can be brought home to enrich daily living in ways not imagined before.

What Happens to Us on Retreat?

Now that we have discussed the core practices a bit, let's look at what will happen as we combine these in a structured routine when we go on a retreat. There are two basic differences from our practice at home, which can lead to the dramatic results:

- We may be doing more practice sessions than at home, and this takes us much deeper into inner silence.

- Whether we are doing more sessions or not, we are going much deeper into stillness due to group practice in a structured way, guided by the retreat leaders.

These two dynamics, while not the only factors at play, are the main influences producing the powerful effects on a retreat. The bottom line is much more abiding inner silence being cultivated. From this comes a host of experiences that are dependent on the main event of more inner silence being cultivated.

The experiences that do come may be subtle or dramatic, just as experiences we may notice at home and going about our daily activities may sometimes be more dramatic than other times. Interestingly, just sitting and doing our practices each day brings all of this about. On retreat, it is the same process operating in "turbo" mode. It is practices that bring about the experiences, not the other way around. This is why we often say that we will be wise to regard our experiences, no matter how dramatic, as "scenery" going by. As long as we remain clear about causes and effects of practices and experiences, we will always keep the horse of practice in front of the cart of experiences.

This is not difficult when we are on retreat, where we are on a specific schedule of sessions, and we continue with that, regardless of the experiences that may come up, assuming they are digestible. More likely, experiences will be tickling us deep in our joyful inner silence. Much of what happens on a retreat is just plain fun. Then we come to realize that the nature of human spiritual transformation is joy and freedom on this earth plane, and that it is available to anyone who is willing to take the time to cultivate it w/in ourselves.

cultivate it within themselves. If it has not become apparent at home as a result of our daily practice there, it will very likely become apparent when we are on a retreat.

We are all wired for liberation in this life!

Experiences – Signs of Purification and Opening

An important point we have raised often throughout the AYP writings is that experiences are nearly always a symptom of purification and opening within us. This applies to experiences in our external environment also, which are symptomatic of a gradually deepening perception of our surroundings.

What do we mean by a symptom of purification and opening? A simple way to look at it is to consider that practices tend to increase the flow of spiritual energy through our nervous system. When this energy is restricted in some way, there can be a sense of something flowing, or wanting to flow. This can feel like a stuckness (blocked), or like a sensation of discomfort, irritability, ecstatic reverie, compassion, love, harmony, oneness, etc. All of these are indications of something wanting to move, moving, or of having moved. Our perceptions of these things are really dependent on energy moving. Perception is energy moving through our neurobiology, creating an impression that is noticed in awareness.

Interestingly, as we become aware of the process of perception, we will be inclined to identify our "self" less and less with the comings and goings of experience, because we know they are external symptoms of movement coming from much deeper within us, i.e., from pure bliss consciousness that we have been cultivating in our sitting practices. We come to know this inner awareness, or witness, as our self, separate from all the objects of perception. Our awareness is not an object of perception, except symbolically when we think of it, which is not the thing itself. Awareness, or abiding inner silence, is the subject in the ongoing experience of our life. It is awareness we are seeking to expand in our practices and on retreat. The experiences will be there according to the expansion of abiding inner silence, which is the cause of purification and opening.

This is why we have often said that it is best to favor our practice over the experiences. Practices produce enlightenment. Experiences do not.

So when these things are coming up during a retreat, we will do best to take them in stride. Even so, we may be laughing a lot, feeling incredible bliss, and love for those who are with us on the retreat, and for all of humanity and the world. That is how it goes.

But let's get more specific. Here is a list of possible experiences we might notice while we are on retreat:

1. Deep abiding inner silence, noticed as a sort of all-pervading blissful cottony cloud extending in all directions that we are walking around with on the retreat. We might notice a quality of white

light associated with this. We may see it emanating from ourselves or from others. Others may notice it emanating from us.

2. A loving sense of oneness encompassing everyone we are with on the retreat, and for the world in general. This is a taste of the unity we will eventually find to be a full time experience in life.

3. Surges of creative energy and insight that might take the form of revelations, which may or may not be practical revelations. This is why we do not make major decisions, engage in work, or have contact with the outside world while on retreat. Better to wait until we get back home to re-engage fully in our life again. Then our expanding creativity will be flowing more, and always available to us, as the abiding inner silence cultivated on retreat is permeating our daily life.

4. A more profound sense of witnessing than we may have experienced prior to the retreat, meaning a greatly reduced identification with things going on within and around us. This is the foundation of all spiritual progress, and why we are cultivating abiding inner silence for the long term.

5. Some discomfort relating to energy moving through restrictions in the nervous system. There could be some headache, irritability or emotional excesses. If it gets to be too much, it is time to self-pace, and check with our buddy and the retreat leaders for assistance.

6. Deep tiredness that can have us wanting to do nothing but sleep for a whole day. We can do that if the urge to sleep is overwhelming. It is deep purification occurring, and new openings are just around the corner. We should do our best to stay with the retreat schedule, but if the urge to sleep is overwhelming, we can stay in our room. We should advise our buddy if we will not be attending practice sessions, meetings, or meals.

7. Feelings of boundless energy and omnipotence, tempting us to engage in all sorts of physical and mental activity. We should let go of the urge to express outwardly and stay with the retreat schedule as best we can. We will achieve the best results on our retreat that way. There is plenty of time to be more active after the retreat.

8. Bliss, and more bliss, accompanied by spontaneous laughter, and extended periods of the giggles. One of the clearest indications of divine inner silence is spontaneous laughter.

9. Physical movements during practice sessions, and sometimes (rarely) during a meeting or at other times on the retreat. Even if we do not notice this in ourselves, we may notice it happening with someone else. It is a normal expression of purification and opening. Not a prerequisite for progress, but an occasional byproduct. It is particularly common for those who are stabilizing structured samyama practice, particularly with the "Lightness" sutra.

10. A sudden surge of energy that can cause an audible expression in the form of spontaneous vocalized sounds. It is not common, but can happen. If someone shouts out suddenly for no apparent reason in a practice session or meeting, an inner energy surge will be the likely cause.

11. Possible manifestations of clairvoyance, clairaudience, and other forms of refined sensory perception, paranormal abilities, etc. If such perceptions occur, we should take them in stride, and not attempt to engage them beyond simple noticing. In such an elevated environment as on a retreat, where abiding inner silence is being extensively cultivated, it is rare for any such perceptions to be other than of a high vibratory quality.

12. <u>Synergistic happenings and coincidences</u>. We may notice <u>our intentions manifesting naturally in our surroundings</u>. For example, we may casually think of something we would like, and then it appears either immediately or shortly thereafter. This is the samyama effect, where our thoughts and intentions are occurring much more in stillness on retreat, with corresponding results. If it happens, we should take it in stride. As with anything that happens on a retreat, we should <u>avoid too much analys</u>is and just carry on with the schedule. When we get home, we will find a strengthened relationship between our inner silence, intentions, and natural outcomes in everyday living.

13. <u>The occurrence of an overwhelming urge to be silent</u>. If this <u>comes naturally, we can honor it</u>. We should not mentally regiment ourselves into silence on a standard retreat. But if it comes naturally, we can let others know we are not available for much talking by wearing a tag on our shirt indicating our silent mode. If we have signed up for an advanced retreat where silence is being observed, we should follow the guidelines for that provided by the leaders.

[margin note: tags/pins for silence]

All of these symptoms and experiences are signs of inner purification and opening occurring, and we can welcome them as long as our stability and ability to stay with the program are not jeopardized. By staying with the program we will maximize the results that we take home with us. If any symptoms become excessive while on retreat, and we are not sure what to do, we should contact the retreat leaders for assistance with self-pacing and grounding.

We may see lots of lovely scenery (experiences) while we are on retreat. Or we may not. Either way, purification and opening will be happening underneath, as abiding inner silence is doing its work. No matter what our experiences may be, as long as we are comfortably favoring the retreat program, the results will be there.

Uplifting Effects on the Surroundings

Just as we will notice a positive radiating effect from the rise of abiding inner silence within ourselves and among all who are on retreat with us, this affect also goes out into the surroundings for quite a distance. It could be said that the effect reaches around the whole world, and far beyond. While those who are 1000 miles away may not feel the affect of our intensive retreat practice the way the person sitting across from us in the deep meditation hall will, there will be an uplifting effect all the same. So when we sit to meditate, and especially while we are on retreat generating so much more spiritual power in a group, we are uplifting the entire world.

This is an important reason why we encourage everyone to go on retreat several times each year. By doing so, we not only hasten our own evolution, but we also hasten the evolution of all humanity. The divine inner stirring that you and your retreat mates create in people all over the world can be enough to elevate their conduct, and even bring them to seek a daily meditation practice themselves. As others act on the uplifting energy, a snowball effect occurs, where a few people stimulate the process of human spiritual transformation in a few others, and they in turn in a few others, and so on. It is what we mean by "candles lighting candles until all candles are lit."

By deepening our own experience individually and in groups through practices, we are also illuminating everyone everywhere from the inside. The human race and all of existence are connected like that. As we do our practices on retreat, steps leading to an enhanced quality of life are being stimulated everywhere, resulting in positive change on the earth, on the inside, and on the outside. The earth needs it, that's for sure.

It is the radiance of inner silence from a multitude of sources, which is simultaneously the stirring of stillness and the radiance of ecstasy from within everyone.

Lasting Cumulative Benefits

Just as the effects of a retreat have a long reach in distance, so to do they have a long reach in time. While there is a fading that occurs when we get home from a retreat, this is normal as we integrate the abiding inner silence we have cultivated during the retreat into our daily activity. In time, as our activity is enriched, we will notice a gradual reduction in the contrast between abiding inner silence (witnessing) and our daily activity. The two merge to become one, with our daily activity rising in quality as inner silence becomes grounded in our life. That merging will be at a higher level of inner silence integrated in our life than we had before we went on the retreat. That is the lasting cumulative effect.

Baking inner silence into our life after a retreat is similar to how inner silence is baked into our life from our daily practice. The daily practice is the short cycle we are cultivating abiding inner silence with. Retreats provide a long cycle of deeper cultivation and integration. This is why retreats are suggested several times each year, so the long cycle can be renewed, just as we renew the short cycle of our practices twice each day.

As we go through these cycles of going deep in cultivating abiding inner silence, we are gradually loosening our identification with the objects of perception – physical, mental and emotional. This gives rise to a state of freedom in daily living that has been called "enlightenment." It is peace, creativity and happiness through all the ups and downs of life. That is what we are after.

As we go further with integrating inner silence into our life, we can help the process along with additional practices, including mudras, bandhas, samyama, self-inquiry, and additional practices we may be inclined to undertake. Abiding inner silence is the foundation from which all the rest can rise and add to our unfolding liberation. The baseline retreat structure is designed to accommodate these additional practices for those who are doing them. Specialized retreats can also be offered for training in practices beyond the core practices of deep meditation, spinal breathing pranayama and asanas.

Chapter 4 – Bringing it Home

As is also the case with our daily practice, the real benefits of a retreat are not to be found in whatever experiences we might have during practice. Rather, the benefits are going to be found in our daily life. If we can view our entire retreat experience as "practice" and favor that while we are there, then we can gain the most from it when we go back out into our active life.

While we may be inclined to think in terms of the experience we have on retreat and the inspiration that memories of such profound experience can produce, the real payoff will come in what we have when we get home, elevating our work, our family life, and all of our interactions in the world in countless and often invisible ways.

The Rise of Abiding Inner Silence

As we have often mentioned, the rise of abiding inner silence is the key. If we are prudently cultivating this sacred quality within us, all the rest will be taken care of in every other department of our life. As it has been said:

"Seek first the kingdom of heaven, and all the rest will be added…"

Abiding inner silence is the *kingdom*...

This becomes apparent as we move through life with greater presence, more peace, more creativity, more energy, and most important of all, more innate awareness of who and what we are.

The practical benefits of abiding inner silence are far-reaching and come into focus as we learn to work with our expanding awareness. For example, in the AYP writings we discuss the emergence of "relational self-inquiry" which is the ability to inquire about the truth of life *in stillness*, or *the witness*. As we are able to do this, the dynamics for change are in place, and suffering becomes a thing of the past. No longer do we see ourselves as the one who is in pain.

Developing the ability to release intentions in stillness is a key characteristic of samyama, which can be cultivated in daily practice, and later as a natural ability in daily living. Releasing intentions and inquiries in abiding inner silence will transform our life, enabling us to move beyond witness state only, to a condition of stillness "moving" as a divine flow coming through us in all that we do.

This divine flow is unifying, meaning our sense of self becomes universal in all relationships where we are engaging within our physical environment with all persons and objects. All is experienced as a single flow, and that is our *Self*. This is *Unity*. Then we are doing all that we do without doing – living in the world, but not being of the world. It is a joyful existence, a highly effective existence, free from the burdens of attachments and painful imaginings, even while fully engaged, most often for the benefit of others. Their needs naturally become our needs.

And for all of this, we don't have to take anyone's word for it. Let's practice daily and go on retreats every so often. Then we will know from our own direct experience. This is how all spiritual practices should be judged, not only by their promises, but by their results in ordinary daily living.

A Happier Way of Living

Living such a level of freedom is happiness, beyond what we could have imagined. Being it is not the same as imagining it. It is far more. Once our desire inspires us to move into daily practice and the benefit of group practice at periodic retreats, there can be no holding us back from the birthright that is ours for the taking.

There is a spectrum of experiences and realizations that come with arising enlightenment, or "liberation," as it has also been called. The AYP writings explore this in some detail. Whether we choose to study about it or not, the results will be there if we are practicing. If you find that retreats work well for you, and you are inclined to make them a part of your life from time to time, then this small book has served its purpose. Your practice is special, facilitating your own awakening, and the awakening of many others. We do retreats for ourselves, and for everyone. Practice wisely, and enjoy!

The guru is in you.

Further Reading and Support

Yogani is an American spiritual scientist who, for forty years, has been integrating ancient techniques from around the world which cultivate human spiritual transformation. The approach is non-sectarian, and open to all. His books include:

Advanced Yoga Practices – Easy Lessons for Ecstatic Living (Two Volumes)
Two large user-friendly textbooks providing over 400 detailed lessons on the AYP integrated system of practices.

The Secrets of Wilder – A Novel
The story of young Americans discovering and utilizing actual secret practices leading to human spiritual transformation.

The AYP Enlightenment Series
Easy-to-read instruction books on yoga practices, including:

- *Deep Meditation – Pathway to Personal Freedom*
- *Spinal Breathing Pranayama – Journey to Inner Space*
- *Tantra – Discovering the Power of Pre-Orgasmic Sex*
- *Asanas, Mudras and Bandhas – Awakening Ecstatic Kundalini*
- *Samyama – Cultivating Stillness in Action, Siddhis and Miracles*
- *Diet, Shatkarmas and Amaroli – Yogic Nutrition and Cleansing for Health and Spirit*
- *Self-Inquiry – Dawn of the Witness and the End of Suffering*
- *Bhakti and Karma Yoga – The Science of Devotion and Liberation Through Action*
- *Eight Limbs of Yoga – The Structure and Pacing of Self-Directed Spiritual Practice*
- *Retreats – Fast Track to Freedom – A Guide for Leaders and Practitioners*
- *Liberation – The Fruition of Yoga*

For up-to-date information on the writings of Yogani, and for the free *AYP Support Forums*, please visit:

www.advancedyogapractices.com